Carreg Las
&
other work

John
Jones

THE COLLECTIVE PRESS

Cataloguing In Publication
Data for this book is available from the British
Library

ISBN 1 899449 80 9

Published with the financial support of the
Arts Council of Wales.

Graphic art by John Jones
except;* *Deidre of the Sorrows (see acknowledgements)*
Please note that due to financial considerations the
images in this book are reproduced in 'greyscale'
but can be viewed in full colour @
'www.blackmountainpoet.com'

Main Typefaces;
TW Cen MT
Trebuchet MS
Moon
Braille

Printed and bound in Great Britain by
The Bath Press, Bath.

CΛ\\Γꞃ

LΛ/

S

O—oΓ\ ∩O\<

foreword

This exquisite book demands activity from its reader. We are asked
to respond in many ways: to puzzle out the moon font, to imagine
touch as our only conduit to the written word, to negotiate the
difficult spaces between the artwork, the poems and the reader. We
have to trust these spaces, understanding that what is not said is as
important as what is said. Yet the poems are full of sounds, full too,
of textures as well as finely-drawn images.   Our senses become
heightened as we read. Everything here is interconnected, literally
and metaphorically. Meaning is often revealed through the discovery
of surprising juxtapositions, so we can

> *"hear the drone of a*
> *bee*
> *and think it*
> *machine"*

But connection is not easy. The vodafone may be turned off, the boys
have only one line they can say, the girls are too busy dancing with
each other to listen, the land is difficult and disappointing, full of
molehills.

John Jones invites us to try again. To understand that "everything
bleeds" - perhaps a pointed riposte to Alice Cooper's allegedly femi-
nist song "Only Women Bleed" - and, by the end of the book, we are
up to our ankles in male blood. Not a symbolic castration, so feared
by some men in this post-feminist age, but a real one; of a horse. For
such a job we are better, John Jones tells us, not to be "wearing
shoes", better to be in touch with the reality of lifeblood. To live,

to connect, to be part of the world we must be open and, indeed, vulnerable, to the truth about blood which symbolises both life and death, to the beauty of "sharp hilltops", to the voices of our ancestors and ourselves when we cross over that edge into a place where anything might happen.

This book, touched with mortality, celebrates the business of being alive, reminds us "we're a long time dead". John Jones is asking us to live with our shoes off. Not to walk away from the lapis horse but to acknowledge the "exchange between hearts", the importance of the cyclical nature of things, the fact that "there is strength here; all we have to do is find it". - and, sometimes to take a gun with us, just in case.

Alicia Stubbersfield

Acknowledgements & Afterthoughts

Some of these poems first appeared in
'Planet' (the Welsh Internationalist), 'Scintilla' an annual publication
of the Usk Valley Vaughan Association and 'Over Milk Wood' an
anthology of Welsh Poets in support of the Wallich Clifford
Community.

Special thanks go to the literature department of the Welsh Arts
Council for their support and Arts Council bursary during 1999,
without which the main body of this work may never have been
completed.

Thanks also go to the Museum of Scottish Arts
for permission to use the charcoal drawing
' Deidre of the Sorrows' by John Duncan.

Maps are with the kind permission of the copyright holder and come
from the publication
'The Prehistoric Landscapes of the Eastern Black Mountains'
Published by Archaeopress
ISBN 1 84171 057 1

In my early days a group of 'teachers', believing me 'dyslexic',
asked if I knew what that meant. Answering "no" I was advised to
"check it out in a dictionary".
Still finding difficulty taking such advice I wish to thank all those who
were kind enough to proof read this book.

.

Please note

The author would like to take this opportunity to acknowledge the creative works of the following people which were encountered during the period of the W.A.C. bursary and up to the time of this work's completion prior to publication. (It is self evident that no artist works in complete isolation, no matter how remote his existence. It may be of interest to the reader, therefore, that some of the following may have had an influence, in some part, on the final draft.)

Shawn Mullins;
for the album 'Soul's Core'.

Richard Brautigan;
for the short stories 'Revenge of the Lawn'

Luka Bloom;
for the songs 'Sanctuary' & 'Diamond Mountain'

Tom Petty;
for 'Room at the Top' & 'Rhino Skin'.

Cormac McCarthy;
for the book 'Suttree' and many others

the voice of
Fiona Bryant
(Mezzo-soprano)

&
for my children's drawings
which are a constant source of wonder

·

We place marks in time,
way points in an open field, some guide, some touchstone.
This then my marker for a new time.

I believe this Earth, a living entity, is mirrored in the world I experience as
a stockman. Major movement, the progression of life itself, held in the
smallest of things.

Life, the wondrous, the unthinkable, spins the mind,
the soul's destination.
Some snake on the hill where the sun strikes first
takes heat from rock.
The certainty of what it does brings light to the artist,
reflects to the art.

I became aware of a poetry that does not reside exclusively within
'the poem'.
In short, on a life that stems from and is altered by some
poetic thought.

This realisation, combined with the question 'What is this poem to do?'
had a much deeper effect than I first thought, the discovery of actual
space within the 'now'. The soul then, free of its working parameters,
lets the 'poetic' affect its inner core.

Here I stand then, in a world where life is structured in order to make it 'friendly' but how do we feel the earth if we cover it over? How will we break the boundaries of awareness when we have nothing left to be aware of? How do we live if we bury our hearts? When we have polluted the sky with light and taken away the stars where will our souls turn?

I have found liminal space within poetry itself by
discovering the dimensions of 'my space'
within time and the real world.

Is this then

a chain

these unconnected events?

Content

event		page
	foreword	06
	acknowledgements	08
one	the red radio	19
two	machine	21
three	never did	22
four	no pretty boy in here	23
five	up	24
six	blackthorn	25
seven	wanted *(one angel)*	26
☯	carreg las	27
saith	shss; like a bullet	54
chwech	big	55
pump	lapis horse	56
pedwar	verbalising silence	57
tri	from the killing gate	58
dau	river	60
un	caspian's nuts	61
	notes	65
	maps	70

13

at the cut off point

everything bleeds

'to challenge the confines of physical space or
moral space while within the boundaries
of a poem that
doesn't offer a formal start
or the finality of an end game'

(above)
Nucleus of original concept
submitted in bursary
application.

story = history
storey = floor

Third stor(e)y,

   my bedroom.

      One window . . . and that saw nothing most times.

Just a flat roof where the old crows walked

top of a chain-store-shop that got itself fragmented way back.

     Way back though the summers . . well they were different.

             Yeah, I know, but hell man they were!

Break times too! I waited for break times, knew when they were coming.

Waited by my window.   Couldn't see that one on the flat-roof though.

           First thing I'd see was the red radio.

A red radio with a big gold dial like the sun.   W o w !   That was some

radio.

First off, out would come the radio, it was always on. . . . . . Rock & Roll!

Used it like disinfectant they did, to clean the roof down, frighten away the

ghosts of those who built it.   The ghosts of Chapel men I guess.   They and theirs

seem to have done most things 'round here.   Think they didn't approve of Rock

& Roll, rather play their organ and, Jesus, their organ used to frighten me!

Always best to frighten them first . . . . with that red radio.

Then . . . . . to hold it . . . . . the guys appeared

through the window I couldn't see . . . they were only extras.

               Never noticed them much,

like those real heavy drapes, those eyelids over the silver screen just before the

lights went down, they drew apart . . . you noticed . . . but that's about all.

Never heard anyone say wow! Look at them drapes.

         Then the girls came,

crisp and clean in whites. Looking to me as if they'd just stepped out of the cool

room but that was real daft, the cool room was a small place and always broke

down, especially on hot days like these.

Of course I knew them all by name and they knew me but I was just a boy then

and lived next door.   I guess they thought me cute with my blonde curls and big

blue eyes.

Why don't cute kids think they're cute too?

Yeah, I knew them all, but not so I'd say, and when they were out on the chain -store roof with that red radio I only knew them the way I knew Marilyn Monroe or Scarlet or Valerie Singleton . . guess I had a crush on her way back then.

I'd watch them laughing in the hot sun, waiting for one to melt . . . never did though.

And they'd dance when something special dropped to earth and hit the radio.

They'd all shout "It's a hit" as if they knew.

Then they'd dance . . . . and I wouldn't blink . . . . not even for a second.

The chain store roof would come alive and jive, even though it was only concrete with nothing to cling to, no pillars or posts, just space the surrounds of a three storey drop.

And the dancers would dance and never fall off.

I watched and never blinked and the radio would just sit there and play . . . . and play as if for all the world . . . . this was it . . . . . what it was made for.

Then one of the drapes would say something and that was that.

The girls, back to the cool room and their usual B movie bit parts.

The guys, staying as drapes but without the movement . . . and that one line.

Last to leave was always the radio with its dial, as if passing through cloud, keeping the ghosts from the dance floor one last time . . . . . 'till everything closed.

I blink again.

That was then. I was a small boy the 'white' girls thought cute. I'd like to think you and me could dance there one day. I'd be content with a walk on part and one line and you could just dance and maybe, if you asked me, I'd have something to cling to.

Tomorrow . . . . . I'm gonna buy me a red radio.

But for now

amongst roses

writing poetry

I smell the gravel dust

from a tractored lane

hear the drone of a

bee

and think it

machine

●

I

never

did

buy

me

that

red

radi

an un

-camera

friendly face

eye splits

looking

like an Inuit's

whale bone

shades

or the nose

bent around

someone's fist

and a jaw that locks

for the same reason

giving cunnilingus

and poetry

problems

in performance

and do I want

the man said

to be the next 'new thang'

blown out

of some proportion

then delivered to the masses

on slippery paper

branches

greening

bear

the dead

leaves

still

to fall

as moving

others

give

dry sound

the day

sharp

hill tops

plain

unspoken

the horse

in thin air

shines

here the end

life

a ridge

the tree line

the very act

of looking down

.

?

sometime

above the line

where the white boned heads

shoot and curl

like arsenic

back high from the bracken sea

and the inter space of pathways

bubble bushes from the mound

I find

the movement slowed

     to almost still

     and sanity firm rooted

     not like us as steel to bone

     but as a skewer

struck through green

       •

one angel

today I caught

a fledgling as it fell

and stood there thinking

bloody hell

what do I do with you

•

At Carreg Las, within the round cairn & at the cist on Mynydd Y Gadair

'The universe proceeds in a straight line. If time were cyclic, Christ would be crucified again and again. There would not be that one perfect and sufficient sacrifice, oblination and satisfaction for the sins of the whole world.'

St. Augustine of Hippo

All that lives belongs to the land, it identifies us for who we are. There is no beginning, no end to this, just a portion of time to share, to exist, to be known.

I am neither Christian or Jew; Muslim, Hindu, wise man or fool. I am all of these and none at all. I have curved time's metal to the hoop and sent it spinning in my soul.

JJ

So this

love

is liminal space

its eastern gap

a door

to the other world

I can't   but enter

inside

I lose

my sense of place

and dreams

hold nothing

the empty seed heads

on the red stalked grass

growing here

curve

•

there is no one   when I call

you   my ancestors

live outside   are long dead

     or away from here

I feel the sun

hear the constant breeze

like the beat of a bird's

wing around my head

smell the berry juice

     crushed

     beneath my feet

     †

Frank is a distant bone

taking readings

measuring

     space

between circle and cairn

     •

I am in this other world

refusing to budge

funny

how death

is not here

in this place

that housed the dead

I feel

neither safe

nor threatened

if this is fate

   will I survive

it is

just a question of time

         •

I remember

exchanging words

on the way here

"we're a long time dead"   we said

I don't

know

if

that's long enough

all sounds are empty

the vodafone I'm calling

may be switched off

.

why is the hill

so hard

when

    its surface

      is not

      solid

       .

I see Frank's head

. . . . distant

his straw hat

white

like a sheep's skull

or an overused metaphor

         amongst stones

     •

he gives me space

time to think

about you

                and he doesn't know

                    you exist to me

only your words

           and I want more

the chamber that makes them

the mouth that speaks

the soul that knows

how their sound

touches mine

      •

he's gone again

measuring some distance

a search

for some

subjective fact

I remain where the dead once lay

I am not certain

if I'll ever make it back

the vodafone I've been calling

may be switched off

•

does an hour pass

•

I will burn here

I can feel it

                                        tighten my skin

as once

it tightened flesh

on long

                    shifted
                                    bones

                    a breeze

remains

                    a red rucksack

breaking the green

such

                                    purple ground

                        .

Frank is lost

in the measurement

        of time

will I ever get back from here

will you sing

my praise

in the land of giants

        if I've gone

or will my name

stick in your throat

or slip

    down

      your

        face

          when a tear falls

•

I am still

within the circle's space

and nothing

nothing of the other world

the vodafone I've been calling

may be switched off

.

I will endure this

there is strength here

in the land that bore me

and dead men

can endure much pain

.

the breeze is constant

nothing else

much

moves

the empty heads of dreams

so why should I

what is my life

amongst this

I am not stone

to be moved aside

or good land

to be made

infertile

•

my soul

will not lie here

if love is to be won

and you are trapped

in some other world

I will begin again

wasn't that the start

some understanding

an exchange between

hearts

if I've lost you

then I'll find you

make you mine again

•

this is the place

where they bring the dead

            I am not dead yet

the vodafone I've been calling

may be switched off

            •

at the doorway

one song

a singer

      this earth

not yet

    not yet

words must flow   between us

the vodafone   I've been calling

must be replaced   by the touch of skin

                  I will not be turned off

                    we are a long time dead

not yet

    not yet

there is a soul to call back

and somewhere

a heart

. . . tiredness . . .

these words have taken all to make

. . . . my memory . . . . a small

petrified thing . . . . a shadow to hide

. . . . better then . . . to be placed

in a cist and sealed there . . . . . .

. . . .

for time doesn't heal anymore, just

fades the edge like quicklime on a

pit of broken bones.

But time still . . . . does pass.

This is the land that bred us after all

and who are we!   What is this

sorrow but the stones we touch or

rest upon.   There is strength here;

all we have to do

is find it.   .

I take down gun today, with the sun cooling in clouds beyond the western hills. To shoot nothing you understand, just hold.

Damn, this gun's got a fine shape to it and the wood, as long as it's not on one of these 'lately weapons', is always chosen. I like that. The way someone makes a difference to a different kind of thing.

We cross the yard, clean by rain, this gun and me. Moving quietly beyond the back buildings, stone red in the blood-wash.

I slide a bullet in the breach knowing, less I come on a cougar or something , I'll slide it out again when I get back. Chance of cougars being remote in these here Black Hills.

Me and gun just walk the grass. I finger its warm curves and sometimes scope on a horse or ram moving slowly down through the half-light of trees. When I get to where I'm going, and I just haven't worked out where that is yet, I'm gonna sit and rest this Springfield on my knees and take a look at England.

I won't see it from where I'll be, just Holy Mountain, the Lion Hill, near by and east, painted red with the same wash that marks . . . . . . just the tops of everything by now.

I don't need to I guess.

I already have the bullet

     and the heart to use it.

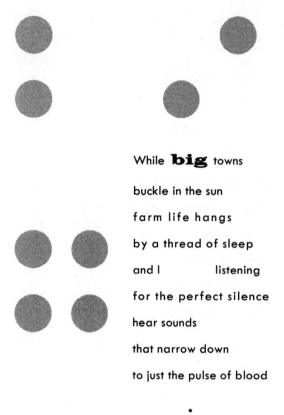

While **big** towns

buckle in the sun

farm life hangs

by a thread of sleep

and I   listening

for the perfect silence

hear sounds

that narrow down

to just the pulse of blood

.

the horse I never bought

was blue

shot through with gold

and bold

as a stallion's eye

in June

sipping apple tea

I grappled with its purchase

shook hands

with a Turkoman

and on the coast

of the Caspian Sea

walked away

as if to say

this sky

this sea

are blue enough

for me   today

on looking back

this horse was more

than smuggled stone

carried here by men

on mountain roads

less civilised than mine

and worth in spillage

just a little of my blood

I can make a minute

hear within this shot

of sun where geese

with young tear grass

from the earth's scalp

I can fill this time

with the never noticed

noise they make

when buzzards pass

or heavy bees drone by

and I can hear feathers form

a drum above young down

and sound vibrate

in the wing space

sheltered there

and I regret that sounds like these

will soon be lost to rain

and the memories of paper

(Pentwyn Hill Fort - tribal stronghold and eastern outpost of the Silures)

'Come and sit where the pine stands high above the long valley. Look here and mark
you well for this be an old land.'

Once the men of Ergyng lived down there, first into battle and
last to leave by right and that right written down by Norman hands into
some great, fat-arsed book . . . . and kept there.

This, as far as we go today, I am the blood upon the blood-
lands and this the edge.

The Saxons had a word for us, my kind, Wealas, a foreigner.
'Welsh' they now say 'you're Welsh', a word to cull us from the heart
land. An insufficient crime for here I stand on this far edge; . . . . . . and
all is silent here . . . . . . no sound but sign . . . . some distant diesel
smoke.

A wagon much like mine works its way back along the dirt track.
The woman at the wheel, unkempt hair and tired hands, flattens molehills
by design.

I know her vaguely. She gave me tea one time after walking
down from Carreg Las. Her man has left, had enough of bitching,
enough of explaining why the farm runs down.

She makes another pass along the track. Her man would have
done this with strychnine but she . . . . . . hasn't got the bottle anymore.
Is just too tired to look.

Far off in town 'learned men' fight over 'just cause' and 'possession rights'. Up here I watch a woman driving molehills back to earth. In the downed ground bodies break and tunnels flatten back . . .
. . . . . 'till all remains as nothing ever passed it by.

She readjusts her seat and smokes the diesel.
I am sprung from Silures and this my edge.
I have no concern for moles.

once I was

as high

        headed

     as a falling stream

    passing over stones

     not stopping

   to move

any but the smallest

from amongst

the rocks turned

    smooth

now I'm almost silent

with the silt I bear

but the songs

that roar

within me

moved mountains

a castration

The first time you see a horse bleed, really bleed, you think 'fuck'.

You get used to it.

They can bleed like this forever.

At least until their lips turn blue.

You think 'fuck', looking to see the depth of blood, looking down, astounded

to see what you'll find there, see if it's over your shoes.

Really . . . . . when you're doing this . . . you shouldn't be wearing shoes.

/ᒣΛLL −ΛL< ΛN⊃ I−/ Iᒣ˓LICΛ−ION/

I ᒣΓN−ION
oΓ\ ΓJΓ/
Λ\Γ ᒐLUΓ
LI<Γ −oΓ /<J I/ ᒐLUΓ
∩oΓN −oΓ /UN LIᑎo−
/oINΓ/
/oΓ /oo∩/ ᒣΓ
O−oΓ\ ᒐLUΓ/
Λ\OUN⊃ −oΓ \OOᒣ
ᒐ\I/−OL ᑎLΛ//
Λ ˓ΓN ΛN⊃ CLI˓
oΓ\ −ΓΓ˗/oI\−
Γ\Γ/o ΛN⊃ LIᑎo−
/UNLI−
∩oΓ\Γ −oΓ /UN LIᑎo−/
/−\UᑎᑎLINᑎ
ΓO\ ᒣO\Γ
∩I/oINᑎ
−oΛ− ΓVΓ\J−oINᑎ ∩Γ\Γ ᒐLUΓ
I OΓΓΓ\ ᒣJ O∩N ΓJΓ/ /ΛJINᑎ
⊃Λ⊃⊃IΓ/ Λ\Γ ᒐLUΓ −OO
/oΓ /ΛJ/
Γᒣ˓oΛ−ICΛLLJ
NO
−oΓJ NO−
⊃Λ⊃⊃J
JOU\/ Λ\Γ ᑎ\ΓJ
LI<Γ Λ ∩OLΓ/

It's difficult to explain how a period of intense writing can benefit an artist. How it creates its own life force, gives its own direction, supplies both map and compass. These journeys, created, are sometimes like strange fruit. They ripen and fall in their own time, grow into their own shape and find their own way of reaching light. We start each with only one certainty, to begin . . . we first must leave. If we have a destination, we can never be sure of reaching it, never be sure of what we'll see or find along the way. How it will change us, this time we spend as travellers.

The W.A.C. bursary from which this work stems has been such a journey, a way of seeking light. It provided a certain freedom, the single mindedness necessary for work like this. As an artist it gave me the wider canvas to work from. To show my concerns with space and time and the soul of things that live there.

This then, the evidence, the traveller's journal, the best way to show how such a bursary has affected my life, my art.

The work progresses, the journey, never ending, offers strange fruit to the traveller. I still have faith in the people I found there, the reasons and the hopes I began with. I have however, left part of 'me' along the way, the price of the traveller I suppose.

I hope someone finds something to remember in these, my traces, the marks I leave.

Good journeys.

John 2001
Jones

Notes on Carreg Las

Liminal space;

an archaeological term describing a place between spaces, worlds or conditions. In the Early Bronze Age, ring cairns and stone circles like Carrreg Las acted as liminal spaces between this world and the Otherworld. The body of a dead person may have been placed within the circle prior to burial, marking his or her transition between the world of the living and the Otherworld of the dead. The circle is the liminal space in which the two worlds meet.

Mynydd Y Gadair;

translated from the old Welsh to be 'mountain of the fort' or 'seat of power', now taken to mean 'mountain of the chair' and shown in maps on page 68 as Hatterall Hill.

vodafone;

at the time of writing, this was claimed to be the UK's favourite mobile phone network.

cist;

a small chamber where the bones of the dead rest after leaving the circle.

Carreg Las;

translated from Welsh to mean;
'ring of blue stones'

Frank;

> a professional archaeologist.

drawing;

> *(page 27)* ; Deirdre of the Sorrows - black chalk by John Duncan 1866 - 1945 with the kind permission of The National Galleries of Scotland.

Otherworld;

> in Celtic reality, the other world runs parallel to this world but time is different there. It could be entered at various liminal spaces e.g. At the ford through a river, at gateways, wells, burial mounds etc. etc. Invariably those returning found this world to be aged while only away but a day in the 'otherworld'.

Place names;

> Many Welsh place-names are feminine nouns preceded by the article *y* ("the") which causes the first letter of the name to soften (or "mutate") e.g. *Carreg* ("rock" or "stone") becomes *Y Garreg*. In many cases, the article is dropped, but is still implicit (it's a Celtic thing!) and the mutation remains e.g. *Garreg Las* ("the blue, grey or green rock"). Sometimes, the mutation occurs even though there is no article implied (an even more Celtic thing!). Just to add to the confusion, the adjective *glas*, though usually used nowadays to mean "blue", could in Old and Middle Welsh mean "blue", "grey" or "green". The same is true in Gaelic - perhaps our common ancestors were colour-blind - or maybe its just another Celtic thing!

This explanation extracted with menaces Mon. 24/09/2001 20:16

notes on 'other work'

machine;

written between performances at the Listowel literature festival, Ireland.

no pretty boys in here;

after an interview with a reviewer who attended a reading to celebrate the opening of a collaborative work with the inner landscape group of artists. An exhibition of paintings and poetry held under the banner of the Hay on Wye literature festival May 2000.

up;

from a series of linked poems known as 'predator poems' some of which have been published in 'Scintilla'.

Shsss - like a bullet;

'Springfield' is a make of a rifle, earlier models playing a prominent part in the American Civil war. This work later published in Planet.

lapis horse;

after an impromptu performance at Ephesus, Turkey and following negotiations with a smuggler of lapis lazuli while en route to give readings for The British Council in Athens and Milan.

verbalising silence;

one of the 'predator poems' which appeared in 'Scintilla 3'

from the killing gate;

below Carreg Las there is the remains of a Silures hill fort at a place known as Pentwyn. Its main entrance was protected by large defensive banks which form the shape of a bull's horn forcing would be attackers into an area known as the killing ground. This poem was written after a discussion on *'Welshness'*. The work later published in Planet

river;

in response to a lecture at a conference held by the Usk Valley Vaughan Association during the summer of 1999 and of the work, constructive criticism and friendship of Anne Cluysenaar.

Caspian's nuts;

A castration is a relatively bloodless affair unless problems develop which, as in this case, resulted in a 'spurter' (a fine spray of blood, under pressure in the 'sack', which continued for many hours)

Information on Braille & Moon fonts can be found at;

www.rnib.org.uk

&

www.moon.co.uk

please note that in this publication the method known as 'ploughing' has not been followed when using either of the fonts mentioned above.

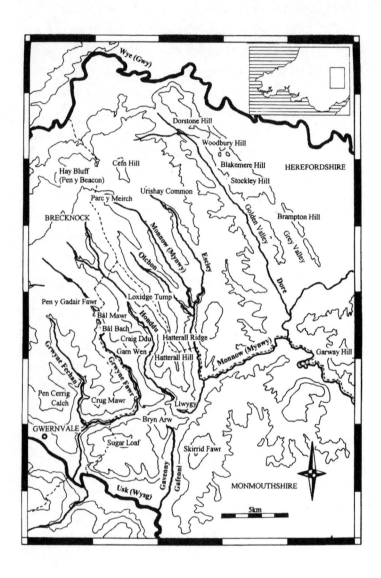

Wye (Gwy)

Dorstone Hill

Woodbury Hill

Cefn Hill

Blakemere Hill

HEREFORDSHIRE

Hay Bluff
(Pen y Beacon)

Stockley Hill

Urishay Common

Parc y Meirch

Brampton Hill

BRECKNOCK

Golden Valley

Grey Valley

Olchon

Monnow (Mynwy)

Exeley

Dore

Pen y Gadair Fawr

Loxidge Tump

Honddu

Bâl Mawr

Bâl Bach

Craig Ddu

Hatterall Ridge

Garn Wen

Hatterall Hill

Monnow (Mynwy)

Garway Hill

Grwyne Fechan

Grwyne Fawr

Pen Cerrig
Calch

Crug Mawr

Llwygy

Bryn Arw

GWERNVALE

Sugar Loaf

Skirrid Fawr

Gavenny

Gafenni

MONMOUTHSHIRE

Usk (Wysg)

5km

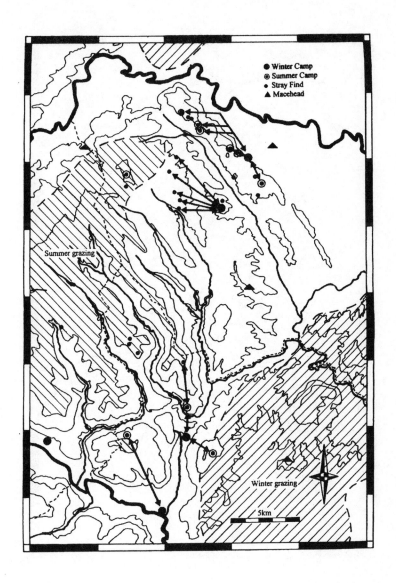

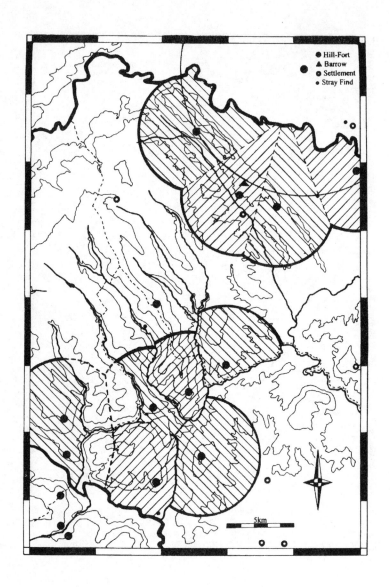

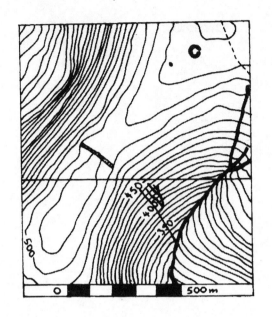

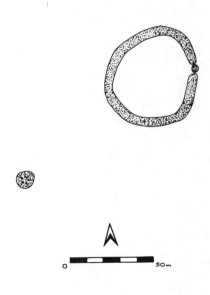

when all this

blood

is dry

and locked

in stone

when all

this love lies

buried

it is not

beyond

the law of

things

to talk

in high

places

to the

bleached

remains

of a dead

man's

bones

†

they may

well be

mine

•

Find
Out More

It is hoped that an appendix to this book will be
available on request from The Collective. It
should also be available for download at the
web address on page 69.
It will set out to 'enlighten' those seeking
publication through The Collective, of the
rigours and processes that their work will be
subject to before it ever reaches
the bookshelf.
It is hoped to use this book 'Carreg las' to help
demonstrate this. Permission is being sought to
include the readers' reports on 'Carreg Las'
commissioned by The Arts Council and
The Collective prior to its publication.
It may, therefore, also be of interest to readers
who wish to see other 'critical' perspectives on
this particular work.
Please ensure you enclose a stamped
addressed envelope when writing to
The Collective.
Alternatively, 'happy surfing'.

Other Collective publications in which
this poet's work appears include;

TILT   ISBN 1-899449-30-2

(Hartill, Hool & Jones)

"Three poets speaking out of a unique landscape"

Tom Pickard

Of Sawn Grain   ISBN 1-899449-35-3

(An anthology of work from The Collective Writers 1993-96)

"Individual visions matter, not because any one vision will change everything
for good or ill but because these visions, collectively, are what society
depends on to evolve."

Anne Cluysenaar

Private People   ISBN 1-899449-50-7

(Ten years in preparation. This is an anthology of work by both
international and home grown talent)

"This book combines celebration and defiance - to bring life, colour and
beauty to an astonished, if not entirely grateful, world"

Frank Olding

please note

Early works include the following books all of which are currently out of
print but may be tracked down, with luck, to a remote corner of some
forgotten book shop.

Tug	isbn	1 899449 10 8
Blind Cwm	isbn	1 899449 00 0
Lucifer's Cradle	isbn	1 899449 05 1

The Collective

welshwriters.com

The Collective is a non-profit-making organisation formed in 1990 to promote and publish contemporary poetry. Funds are raised through a series of poetry events held in and around South Wales. The backing and generosity of fellow writers is a cornerstone of The Collective's success. Vital funding comes from public bodies including the Arts Council of Wales and donations are often received in support of the movement from members of the public. If you would like to contact The Collective to offer help or support then you can write to:

The Co-ordinator
The Chief Editor
or the
Events Organiser.

C/O

The Collective
Penlanlas Farm
Llantilio Pertholey
Y-Fenni
Gwent
NP7 7HN
Wales
UK

fish

⠋⠊⠎⠓

∩|∕o